BADGER RELIGIOUS I

BOOK 2
Christine Moorcroft

Badger Publishing

Badger Publishing Limited
26 Wedgwood Way, Pin Green Industrial Estate,
Stevenage, Hertfordshire SG1 4QF

Telephone: 01438 356907
Fax: 01438 747015.
www.badger-publishing.co.uk
enquiries@badger-publishing.co.uk

First published 2002
ISBN 1 85880 895 2

Text © Christine Moorcroft 2002

Complete work © Badger Publishing Limited 2002

The right of Christine Moorcroft to be identified as author of this Work has been asserted by her in accordance with the Copyright, Designs and Patents Act 1988.

Cover photos:
Icon from a Greek church © Sonia Halliday
(Book 1, *What did Jesus look like?*)
Ganesha © Trip/H Rogers (Book 2, *Hindu Worship – Ganesha*)
Al Aqsa mosque, Jerusalem, Israel © Trip/H Isachar
(Book 3, *The night journey*)
Golden Buddha inside Ganden Monastery, Tibet © Trip/J Sweeny
(Book 4, *Sculpture in Buddhism*)

Publisher: David Jamieson

Editor: Paul Martin

Design: Cathy May

Illustrations © Kathy Baxendale, Juliet Breese, Ray and Corinne Burrows (Beehive Illustration Agency), Josephine Blake (Beehive Illustration Agency)

Photo acknowledgements:
Photographs reproduced with permission from the following copyright holders:
Trip/ H Rogers: 6a-b, 8, 10, 11, 13, 26, 44a/c
Werner Pluess at Gods Artefacts, Sydney: 6c (Shiva)
Corbis UK Ltd: 6d (Vishnu), 39b (plain cross)
Ray Barker: 12
Sonia Halliday: (and B. Knox) 14; 36, 39a (Crucifix)
Christine Moorcroft: 25, 42, 43
Peter Sanders: 44b/e; Trip/T Bognar: 44f

Poster, 42d, provided by the National Hindu Students Forum

Map, 40a, reproduced from Ordnance Survey mapping on behalf of The Controller of Her Majesty's Stationary Office © Crown Copyright. Licence Number MC 100037913.

Extract, 40b, from Durham area *Thomson Local*, reprinted with the kind permission of Thomson Directories

Printed in the UK.

CONTENTS

Hindu worship
Activity 1	Svetaketu, the fig and the salt	**4-5**
Activity 2	One god with many forms	**6-7**
Activity 3	Ganesha	**8-9**
Activity 4	A home shrine	**10-11**
Activity 5	In the mandir	**12-13**

Christmas journeys
Activity 6	Bethlehem	**14-15**
Activity 7	The journey of Mary and Joseph	**16-17**
Activity 8	The journey of the shepherds	**18-19**
Activity 9	The journey of the wise men	**20-21**
Activity 10	Fears	**22-23**

Easter
Activity 11	Palm Sunday	**24-25**
Activity 12	The Last Supper	**26-27**
Activity 13	The Lord's Supper	**28-29**
Activity 14	In the garden of Gethsemane	**30-31**
Activity 15	Peter	**32-33**
Activity 16	The Crucifixtion	**34-35**
Activity 17	The Resurrection	**36-37**
Activity 18	Celebrating Easter	**38-39**

Religions in your neighbourhood
Activity 19	Looking for evidence	**40-41**
Activity 20	Buildings	**42-43**
Activity 21	Caring and sharing	**44-45**
Activity 22	Similarities and differences	**46-47**
Glossary		**48**

1 HINDU WORSHIP

Svetaketu, the fig and the salt

This story is from books of Hindu teaching called the Upanishads (meaning 'to sit down near'). Uddalaka's 24-year-old son Svetaketu has been studying the scriptures since he was 12 and is very proud of his learning. He thinks he knows everything. Uddalaka wants to be sure that he has learned the most important things.

Uddalaka: Svetaketu, did you learn how to hear what cannot be heard, to see what cannot be seen, to know what cannot be known?
Svetaketu: What is that?
Uddalaka: Go and fetch a fig. [Svetaketu cuts a fig from a tree.]
Uddalaka: Cut it open. [Svetaketu cuts open the fig.] What do you see?
Svetaketu: I see tiny seeds.
Uddalaka: Cut open a seed. [Svetaketu cuts a seed.] What do you see there?
Svetaketu: I see nothing.
Uddalaka: The finest essence is in that seed. You cannot see it. Look at the fig tree standing there; the finest essence, which you cannot even see, is its life. This finest essence makes up the self of the whole world. That is the truth. That is the self. That is you.
Svetaketu: Teach me more.
Uddalaka: Put a block of salt into a pot of water. Leave it until tomorrow. [Svetaketu puts a block of salt into a pot of water.]

The next morning...
Uddalaka: Take out the block of salt which you put into the pot of water yesterday. [Svetaketu gropes for the salt. He cannot find it.]
Uddalaka: Taste a drop from the top. [Svetaketu takes a drop from the top and tastes it.] What do you taste?
Svetaketu: Salt.
Uddalaka: Taste a drop from the middle. [Svetaketu takes a drop from the centre and tastes it.] What do you taste?

Svetaketu: Salt.
Uddalaka: Taste a drop from the bottom. *[Svetaketu takes a drop from the bottom and tastes it.]* What do you taste?
Svetaketu: Salt.
Uddalaka: Empty the pot and come back later. *[Svetaketu empties the pot. Exit Svetaketu.]*

Svetaketu and Uddalaka, later in the day…
Uddalaka: Run your finger around the inside of the pot and taste your finger. *[Svetaketu does so.]* What do you taste?
Svetaketu: Salt.
Uddalaka: You did not see the salt, but it was always there. The finest essence is here; it is the self of the whole world. That is the truth. That is the self. That is you.

1 Discuss the story with a partner.
What do you think is 'the finest essence'?
Explain your answer.

What other words could you use for 'the finest essence'?

2 List the places where Uddalaka says 'the finest essence' can be found.
What other places can you think of where it could be found?

3 With your partner, think up another example which Uddalaka could use to help Svetaketu to 'hear what cannot be heard, see what cannot be seen and know what cannot be known'.
Make a flowchart on which to record your ideas.

the finest essence: _____

2 HINDU WORSHIP

One god with many forms

There are many Hindu gods and goddesses. These are four of them.

▶ Vishnu

▲ Sarasvati

▲ Durga

◀ Shiva

WORD-BANK

arrows	mace
bell	shield
bird	skulls
bow	snake
bull	sword
conch shell	tiger
crescent moon	trident
cup	water pot
discus	veena
drum	wheel
lotus flower	

6

1 Look at the pictures of the Hindu gods and goddesses.

Describe what you can see.

Notice any markings on their faces, their skin colour, their arms, what they are carrying and any animals they have.

Use the glossary and the word-bank.

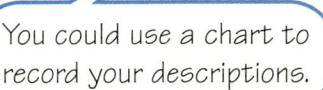

You could use a chart to record your descriptions.

Name	Male or female	Face	Skin colour	Arms	Objects held	Animals and other objects
Vishnu						
Shiva						

2 Which of the descriptions **a** to **d** matches each god or goddess?
How can you tell?

- **a** The goddess of learning. She sits in a lotus flower, playing a veena.
- **b** He created dance. He only opens his third eye when angry, and whatever it looks at burns to ashes. He has matted hair; it holds the river Ganges which flows from his top-knot.
- **c** A fierce, powerful warrior goddess who was born fully-grown.
- **d** The protector of humanity. He sits on the giant snake, Ananta, which has many heads.

3 Many Hindus worship a favourite god or goddess. Some worship different gods or goddesses at different times.

Choose the one you find most interesting.
Find out more about him or her, and write a character study.
Begin by making notes.

Use information books, CDs and websites.

Name of god or goddess		
Words to describe him or her	Evidence from the picture	Evidence from texts

7

3 HINDU WORSHIP

Ganesha

There are many stories about the birth of Ganesha, the son of the goddess Parvati. One story tells how Parvati created a little boy while she was in the bathtub. She collected all the tiny flakes of her skin floating on the water. From her own skin Parvati made a dough and shaped it into a lovely child.

▲ Ganesha

Shiva was hardly ever at home, and Parvati had no one to guard her from danger or to keep out strangers. One day, when the boy was old enough, she asked him to stand guard outside the door while she bathed.

That day Shiva came home. He was taken aback when he found a stranger at his door who would not let him pass. Shiva was furious. He drew his sword and cut off the boy's head.

When Parvati came out to see what all the noise was about she saw her son lying on the ground, bleeding.

Parvati could hardly speak through her sobs, but she told Shiva who he had killed. Shiva wanted to console Parvati. He had an idea; he sent out his troops (the Gana) and told them to cut the head off the first living thing they found asleep facing north.

Soon they found an elephant asleep facing north. They cut off its head and brought it to Shiva. Shiva fixed the elephant's head to the boy's body and brought him back to life.

Shiva named the boy Ganapati (commander of the Gana), and said that in future people would have to worship Ganapati (Ganesha) to make sure that anything they did would turn out well. Shiva made Ganesha the 'remover of obstacles'.

1 Hindus often pray to Ganesha before praying to another god. Talk to a partner about this and re-read the story of Ganesha to find out why.

Use the glossary.

A Hindu prayer to Ganesha

Greetings to you, O Lord Ganesha, born of Parvati, the daughter of the Mountain King, Himalaya, and the great Lord Shiva. O Lord of compassion, you have a single tusk, four arms, a bright mark of vermilion on your forehead, and you travel on a mouse.

Glory, glory, all glory to you O Lord Ganesha.

You give vision to the blind, cleanse the bodies of the leprous, give sons to barren women and wealth to the poor.

Glory, glory, all glory to you O Lord Ganesha.

People offer you betel leaves, blossoms, dry fruits and laddus, while throngs of saints and seers attend you.

Glory, glory, all glory to you O Lord Ganesha.

2 What do the picture, the story and the prayer tell you about Ganesha?

The chart will help.

Ganesha				
What he looks like	How people treat him	His life	What he can do	What people think of him

3 Which of these people might pray to Ganesha, and why?

I'm worried about the exams.

This will be a great holiday!

My mind goes blank whenever I look at this.

4 Why might Hindus find it helpful to have statues and pictures of gods and goddesses?

9

4 HINDU WORSHIP

A home shrine

The photograph shows a shrine in a Hindu home.

WORD-BANK	
arti	lamp
bell	light
god	murti
goddess	puja
incense	water pot
kum-kum powder	

1 How can you tell that this is a special place?

Use the glossary.

2 With a partner, discuss what you can see in the photograph. List the objects and say what they might be for.

3 Find out how a Hindu family looks after the murtis and other objects in the home shrine.

Make notes about what you discover, and write a report:

Caring for murtis: notes

Washing	Dressing	Food and drink	Talking

Caring for murtis: report

Hindus show respect for the murtis (statues and pictures of gods and goddesses) in many different ways.

This photograph shows a puja set. It is used at the beginning of worship at home.

4 List what you can see on the puja tray.

What might you see, hear, smell and taste during puja?

5 How is each object used? Copy and complete the chart:

Purpose	Object
To call the god or goddess to let him or her know that puja is about to begin.	
To wash the statue or picture of the god or goddess and to give as a drink.	
To put a symbol of purity and good health on the worshippers' foreheads.	
To offer milk or water to the god or goddess.	
To symbolise enlightenment (knowledge of what is good).	
To make a pleasant, soothing smell.	

6 Find out more about the arti ceremony. Write instructions for the arti ceremony.

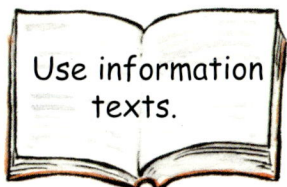

Use information texts.

5 HINDU WORSHIP

In the mandir

The photograph shows a Hindu mandir in Prambanan in India.

1 Make lists of the ways in which the mandir is similar to, and different from, a public building, such as a library or town hall.

Mandir	Ordinary building
decoration	
doorway	
roof	
statues	
walls	

2 How can you tell that the mandir is a special place?

How can you tell that it is a place of worship?

3 Imagine walking from a busy street or market-place and through the doorway of the mandir. Describe the changes which you might see, hear, smell and feel as you go through the doorway.

How might going into the mandir affect your thoughts and feelings?

12

The photograph shows the inside of a Hindu mandir in Bradford in England.

4 How can you tell that the mandir is a place of worship? Describe what you can see.

5 In what ways is the mandir similar to a Hindu home shrine?
Look for objects like those in the home shrine.

See page 10.

6 From the picture, what can you find out about Hindu worship in the mandir? Use information books to find out more about what Hindus do when they worship.

Sounds Smells Tastes

Write a report about worship in the mandir.

6 CHRISTMAS JOURNEYS

Bethlehem

The Church of the Nativity in Bethlehem in Israel was built in the fourth century. It is on the site where Jesus is thought to have been born about two thousand years ago. Beneath the church is the rectangular grotto which is shown in the picture.

The grotto is about 10½ metres long and 3 metres wide. A silver star marks the traditional spot where Jesus was born. On the star are Latin words meaning 'Here Christ was born'. There is a stone manger nearby, which is said to be the one in which the baby Jesus was placed.

Millions of pilgrims have visited this church.

▲ The manger in the Church of the Nativity grotto, Bethlehem.

1 Describe what you can see in the picture.
What do you think the atmosphere might be like in the grotto?

Think about the ways in which the church is special, and different from other churches.

2 How do you feel when you go into a place where something special has happened?
What do you think the pilgrims do, feel and think when they visit the Church of the Nativity?

3 Ask a friend about a special place which he or she has visited.
Ask your friend the questions below.
Make notes about the answers.

Main questions	Extra questions
What makes the place special?	Did something special happen there, or do special things still happen there?
When did you go there?	Was it one visit, or more than one?
What did you do to prepare for the visit?	Did you keep checking how long it would be until you could go? Did you buy anything special? Did you have to save for it?
Who went with you?	What did you talk about on the journey? What kinds of things did you say?
How did you feel before the visit?	Did you feel excited, or impatient?
How did you feel when you arrived?	Was it exciting? What words came to your mind?
What souvenirs do you have of the visit?	What pictures or other things did you bring back?
How do you feel when you think back to the visit?	What are the first words which come into your head when you think about it?

Now answer the same questions when your friend asks you about a visit to a special place.
Swap notes with your friend.
Write a letter to someone else about your visit.

4 Use information books and website videos, pictures and texts to find out about pilgrims going to the Church of the Nativity in Bethlehem at Christmas.
Make notes about what you see and hear, and about the atmosphere in the church.
Write a commentary for a 'virtual pilgrimage'.

7 CHRISTMAS JOURNEYS

The journey of Mary and Joseph

In the days of Herod, king of Judea, there lived a carpenter named Joseph. He was engaged to a young woman named Mary.

The angel Gabriel was sent from God to the town of Nazareth in Galilee. He went into Mary's house and greeted her, calling her 'most favoured one' and saying, "The Lord is with you."

Mary was troubled; she had never seen an angel before, and she wondered why this one had come to see her. He even knew her name; he said, "Do not be afraid, Mary." But she was afraid, especially when he said, "You are going to have a baby, the Son of God. You are to call him Jesus."

"I am the Lord's servant; as you have spoken, so be it," said Mary.

The angel went away. Mary wondered what Joseph would say, but the angel Gabriel went to see him, and told him about the baby. Joseph was not sure if he should marry Mary, even though he wanted to look after her. "Do not be afraid to take Mary as your wife. The child is the Son of God. One day he will save his people from their sins."

That year there was a census – the first of its kind. Everyone in the Roman Empire had to be counted; that included Galilee. The Roman Emperor Augustus sent out an order that everyone must go to the town of his ancestors. Joseph's family came from Bethlehem in Judea – a long way from Nazareth. Mary's baby was due to be born soon, but she and Joseph got ready for the long journey to Bethlehem. They were not rich; all they had for transport was one donkey. Mary rode and Joseph walked.

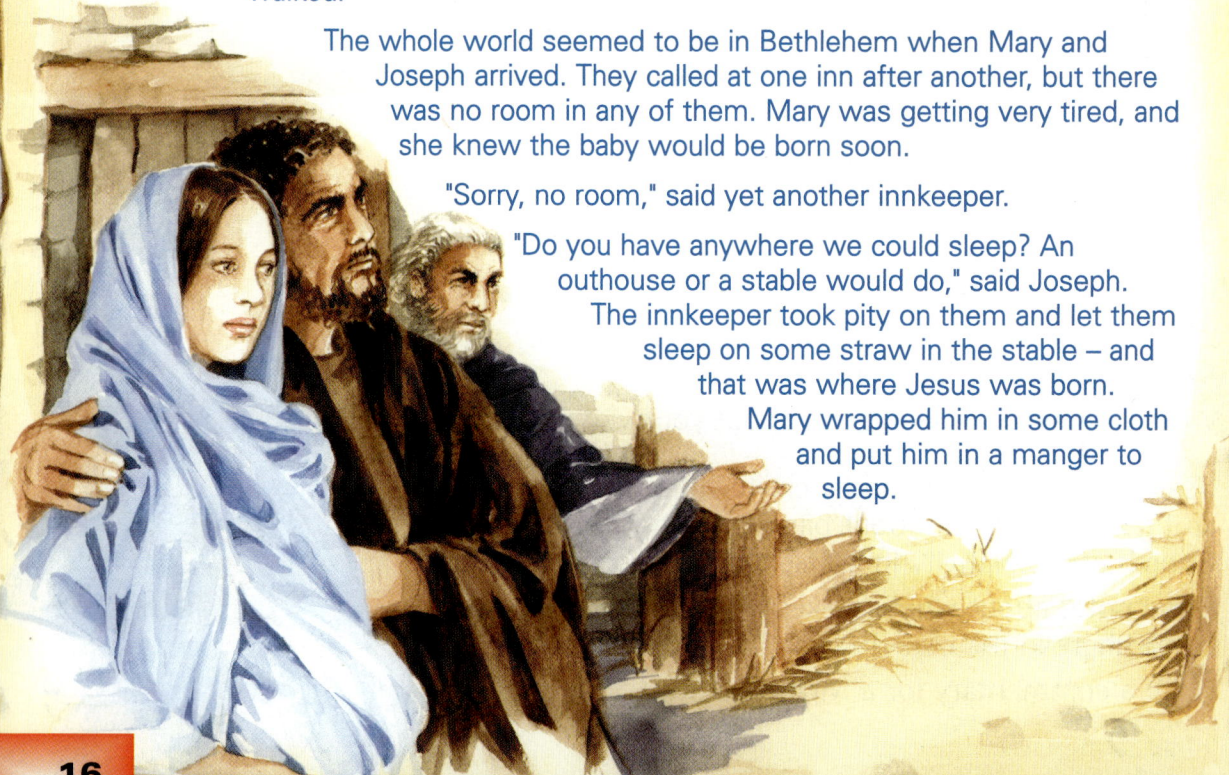

The whole world seemed to be in Bethlehem when Mary and Joseph arrived. They called at one inn after another, but there was no room in any of them. Mary was getting very tired, and she knew the baby would be born soon.

"Sorry, no room," said yet another innkeeper.

"Do you have anywhere we could sleep? An outhouse or a stable would do," said Joseph. The innkeeper took pity on them and let them sleep on some straw in the stable – and that was where Jesus was born. Mary wrapped him in some cloth and put him in a manger to sleep.

1 Why did Mary and Joseph have to go to Bethlehem?

2 List all the things which made the journey and the stay in Bethlehem difficult for Mary and Joseph.

3 The story does not tell of the journey itself. Talk to a friend about what it might have been like.

Make notes. The ideas on the note pad will help.

Work out roughly how many days the journey would have taken.

Write a travel journal for Mary or Joseph.

Look at the map.
Use an atlas and information books, CDs and websites about the land of Israel.

▲ Map of Israel

Weather   Distance
   Roads   conditions
Mary's health, Joseph's feelings
Mary's feelings, Joseph's concern
            for Mary

4 How would Joseph and Mary have felt when they found nowhere to sleep?

Make notes about their feelings.

Compare notes with a partner.

Write the ending of Mary's or Joseph's travel journal. Write about:
- trying one inn after another, looking for somewhere to sleep
- being told that they could sleep in the stable
- the birth of Jesus.

17

8 CHRISTMAS JOURNEYS

The journey of the shepherds

On the night when Jesus was born some shepherds were sitting in a field near Bethlehem, chatting, while keeping watch over their sheep. This was not unusual; they did the same thing most nights.

But this night was different.

The shepherds saw a bright light filling the sky, and then an angel appeared. They saw the glory of God shining all around the angel, and were afraid.

"Do not be afraid," said the angel. "I have good news for you. Great joy is coming to everyone, for today, in the city of David, a deliverer has been born – the Messiah, the Lord. Go and worship him. This is a sign for you: you will see the baby wrapped in cloth, lying in a manger."

As the angel spoke, a host of angels appeared around him, singing the praises of God:

"Glory to God in the highest heaven,
and on earth his peace for those on whom his favour rests."

Then the angels went back to heaven and the bright light faded. The shepherds were still and silent for a while. Then they began to talk about what had happened. "Come, we must go to Bethlehem, the city of David," they said. "We must see this thing which has happened, which the Lord has made known to us."

They hurried to the city and found their way to the stable, where they saw Mary and Joseph; the baby was lying in a manger, just as the angel had said. Other people had begun to arrive, to see the baby.

They told Mary and Joseph about the angel, and what he had said about the child. Everyone was astonished, but Mary listened carefully. She thought about what the shepherds said and she treasured their words.

They gave thanks and praise to God for what they had seen and heard. It had all happened as they had been told by the angel. They went back to their flocks, discussing what had happened.

1 What made the shepherds leave their sheep and go to Bethlehem in the middle of the night? Explain what made them believe the angel.

2 How did the shepherds recognise the place they were looking for in Bethlehem?

Explain what is meant by 'a sign'.

3 The shepherds were ordinary men doing their normal work. Why do you think they were chosen to hear the special news?

If something like that happened tonight, near where you live, what people do you think the angel might visit? What might they do and say?

Explain your answer.

Make notes about the main events of the story.

Using your notes, plan a similar story, set in modern times.

> In those days there were many more shepherds than there are nowadays. Think about the kinds of work which are done by many people today.

> Use a planning chart.

Characters	Setting	Events
Names and descriptions	Description	1 2

Write your story.

> Think about what angels did in the Bible.

4 Angels often appear in the Bible.
Find out more about angels in Christianity:
- re-read the passage and read page 16
- look at paintings of angels
- read or listen to hymns about angels.

What do you think is the role of an angel? How is an angel special?

9 CHRISTMAS JOURNEYS

The journey of the wise men

1 In what ways were the wise men different from the shepherds?

> Think about their learning, their lifestyles and their work.

Read pages 18, 19 and 20.
In what ways did God treat the wise men and the shepherds equally?
What do you think the Bible stories are saying about Jesus?

2 How were the journeys of the shepherds and the wise men similar?

How were they different?

Shepherds' and wise men's journeys	
Similarities	Differences

3 The gifts which the wise men brought to Jesus were very expensive, precious things.

List three presents you would give to a baby.

In what ways are the wise men's gifts unusual?

Describe the sort of person you think would normally have been given expensive, precious things.

In what ways might the gifts have been symbols?

Write your ideas about what this says about Jesus.

frankincense

gold

myrrh

10 CHRISTMAS JOURNEYS

Fears

Joseph had a dream: an angel appeared in his dream, and said to him, "Get up now. Take the child and his mother and flee to Egypt. Stay there until I tell you to leave. Herod is searching for the child, to kill him."

So Joseph rose and woke Mary, and told her about the dream. They set off in the middle of the night for Egypt. They stayed there until they heard that Herod was dead.

Meanwhile Herod waited in vain for the wise men to come back with information about the baby who was to be king of the Jews. He had been tricked. He was furious; he called his men and told them to kill all the children in Bethlehem up to the age of two. He was using information from the wise men to work out how old Jesus must be by then.

When Herod died an angel again visited Joseph in a dream, and said, "Rise up and take the child and his mother to the land of Israel, for the men who threatened his life are now dead."

So Mary and Joseph set off home to Nazareth.

WORD-BANK

anger	jealousy
anguish	joy
bitterness	relief
concern	terror
dread	threat
emotion	tiredness
fear	trouble
happiness	weariness
insecurity	worry

1 Talk to a partner about why Herod wanted to kill Jesus.
How did Herod feel when he first heard about Jesus from the wise men?
How did he feel while he was waiting for the wise men to return?

2 How did Joseph and Mary feel when the angel told them to leave Bethlehem?

How did they feel when the angel came to say that it was safe to go back home?

3 Think about other people who have had to flee from their homes because of fear of being harmed.
Talk to a partner, and make notes.
Find out more from:
- newspapers
- news websites
- television and radio news.

Think about people who have been in the news.

Make notes:

People	Country	Why they fled	Where they went to	What happened when they got there

11 EASTER

Palm Sunday

1 What is happening in the pictures?
How can you tell that someone important is arriving?

2 Think of a time when you have watched an event like these, on television or in real-life.
What was the event, and who was the person (or who were the people)?
What was the feeling among the waiting crowd?
List the kinds of things they said and did.
How did the news spread that the person was arriving (even if he or she could not yet be seen by everyone)?

3 How did the atmosphere in the crowd change once the person came into sight?
What did people do and say?
What feelings did they show?

4 What are the people in the picture doing?
Describe their feelings.
Explain how you can tell how the people feel.
What kind of thing might be about to happen?

> The event in the picture is told in the New Testament of the Bible.
>
> The people in Jerusalem had heard that Jesus was coming. They were waiting for him. As he rode into the town on a donkey the crowd greeted him excitedly, welcoming him with cries of "Blessings on him who comes in the name of the Lord!" and "Hosanna in the heavens!"
>
> Some people threw their cloaks onto the road to form a carpet for Jesus. Others cut branches from palm trees and covered the ground with them.

The festival of Palm Sunday is celebrated in Christian churches on a Sunday between 21 March and 8 April. Its date is worked out from the full moon on or after 21 March.

Worshippers at many Christian churches are given palm crosses in memory of the palm leaves which people placed on the road when Jesus entered Jerusalem.

5 Palm Sunday is the first day of Holy Week for Christians. Find out what Holy Week means.

▲ A palm cross

12 EASTER

The Last Supper

▲ The Last Supper, stained glass window in Bambridge Protestant Cathedral, County Down, Northern Ireland.

Jesus and his disciples were on their way to Jerusalem. They stopped near the Mount of Olives to celebrate the Passover.

Jesus' disciples asked him where he wanted to eat the Passover meal. He sent two of them to see to it, saying, "Go into the city; a man carrying a jar of water will meet you. Follow him. Whichever house he goes into, tell the owner of that house that the Master says, "Where is my guest room where I may eat the Passover with my disciples?" He will show you a large room upstairs, with a table and chairs. Prepare our table there."

So the disciples went into the city and found things just as Jesus had told them; and they prepared the Passover meal.

In the evening, Jesus came to the house with his twelve disciples. While they were at the table, Jesus said, "One of you eating with me will betray me."

This shocked and upset them. One by one they said, "Surely not I?" Jesus said, "It is one of the twelve, one who dips his hand with me into the bowl."

While they were eating, Jesus took bread and gave thanks to God. He broke the bread, gave them a piece each and said, "Take this bread and eat. It is my body."

Jesus picked up the cup and gave thanks to God. Then he passed it to each of them. He said, "Drink from it, all of you. This is my blood, the blood of the covenant. It is poured out for many to forgive their sins. I tell you, from now on I will not drink of this fruit of the vine until I drink it with you in my Father's kingdom."

They sang the Passover hymn. Then they went out to the Mount of Olives.

WORD-BANK

celebrating	quiet
happy	sad
jolly	sharing
lively	symbol
noisy	thoughtful
peaceful	unhappy

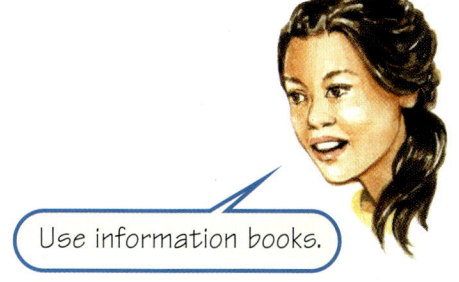

Use information books.

1 Look at the picture. What is happening?
Is it an ordinary meal or a special one?
How can you tell?

2 What were Jesus and his disciples celebrating?
Find out which people celebrate this today, and why.

3 Jesus knew that he was going to be captured and killed.
Talk to a partner about why he did not try to escape.
Which words in the story tell you this?

4 How did the disciples feel when Jesus said that one of them would betray him?
Write about the feelings of the disciples:
- those who would not betray Jesus
- the one who would betray him.

5 During the meal, what two special things did Jesus do?

13 EASTER

The Lord's Supper

The picture shows an altar table in a Christian church. It is ready for a church service called Communion or the Eucharist. The service is also called the Lord's Supper.

1 List the things you can see on the table.
How can you tell that this table is in a Christian church?

2 Look at the picture on page 26 and read the story on pages 26–27.
What links does the picture on this page have with the Last Supper which Jesus shared with his disciples?

Object	Links with the Last Supper

3 Look up the meanings of Communion, Eucharist and Lord's Supper.
Write what they mean.

As the minister gives each worshipper a piece of bread, he or she says, "The body of Christ," and with the wine, "The blood of Christ".

4 How does the Communion service commemorate the Last Supper?

What might Christians think about during the service?

Which words in the prayer show that the Eucharist brings Christians close to Jesus?

5 Interview a Christian to find out what the Eucharist means to him or her.

Write the questions you will ask.

You could ask what happens during the service, what each part of the service means and why it is important.

*Most merciful Lord
your love compels us to come in
Our hands were unclean,
our hearts were unprepared;
we were not fit even to eat the
crumbs from under your table.
But you, Lord, are the God of
our salvation, and share your
bread with sinners.
So cleanse and feed us with
the precious body of your Son
that he may live in us
and we in him;
and that we with the whole
company of Christ may sit
and eat in your Kingdom.
Amen.*

▲ A prayer from a Communion service.

14 EASTER

In the garden of Gethsemane

After the Passover meal, Jesus and his disciples went to the garden of Gethsemane on the Mount of Olives.

The word-bank might help.

1 Jesus knew that he was going to be killed. That was his role, as Messiah.
What kinds of things do you think he might have prayed?

Talk to a partner about how Jesus might have felt as he prayed. Make a note of your ideas.
Read the recounts in the Bible: Matthew 26:36–45, Mark 14:32–41, Luke 22:39–46.
Compare them with your notes.

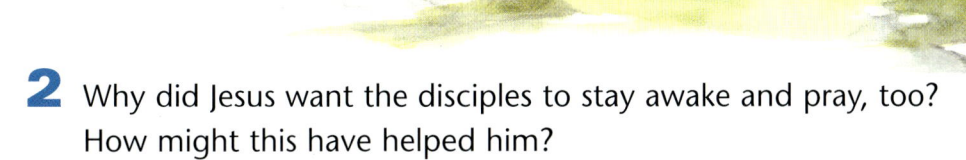

2 Why did Jesus want the disciples to stay awake and pray, too?
How might this have helped him?

3 Did the disciples act as good friends to Jesus?
Write on a chart.

Think about what you would like your friends to do when you face something difficult.

The disciples' actions

Showing friendship	Not showing friendship

4 Discuss with your partner how the disciples might have felt that night. Make a note of your ideas.

WORD-BANK

accepted	dread	guilty	shame
accepting	fear	horrified	sorrow
afraid	forgive	horror	terrified
ashamed	forgiving	knowing	terror
disappointed	grief	sad	worried
disappointment	guilt	sadness	worry

15 EASTER

Peter

At the Passover meal, Jesus had said to Peter, "For you, I have prayed that your faith may not fail. You must give strength to your brothers."

Peter replied, "Lord, I am ready to go with you to prison and to death."

"I tell you, Peter, that the cock will not crow tonight before you have three times denied that you knew me."

This is what happened after Jesus was captured by the crowd.

Jesus was led away from the garden of Gethsemane to the house of Caiaphas the High Priest. Peter followed, but kept his distance. After Jesus was taken into the house, some of the crowd lit a fire in the courtyard. Peter sat among them.

A woman saw Peter, and said, "You were there with Jesus."

"I do not know what you mean," said Peter.

A little later, someone else said, "This man was with Jesus of Nazareth."

Once again, Peter denied it, saying, "I do not know the man."

Shortly afterwards some bystanders came up and said to Peter, "We are sure you are one of them; your accent gives you away."

Peter cursed them and shouted, "I do not know him."

Then the cock crowed. Peter remembered what Jesus had said.

He went out of the courtyard and wept bitterly.

1 Make notes about what Peter said at different times in the story.
Add notes about how Peter felt at these times.

What Peter said	The person he was speaking to	How he felt

2 Was Peter telling the truth when he told Jesus that he was ready to be arrested with him and even to die with him?

Why do you think this?

Why did he not keep his word, but ran away like the other disciples?

3 Peter said that he would never deny knowing Jesus. Did he mean it?

What makes it difficult for people to act on what they believe is right?

Think about other examples.

Make notes about them on a chart:

Belief	Acting on beliefs	Acting against beliefs	Why people do not always act on their beliefs

What do you think made Peter deny that he knew Jesus?

What made him realise what he had done?

How did he feel when he realised what he had done? Use evidence from the story.

Predict what Peter might do in the future, and why.

33

16 EASTER

The Crucifixion

The chief priests tried to find a charge on which to have Jesus killed. They questioned him about many things which people said he had done. Jesus did not answer. Then the High Priest said, "By the living God I charge you to tell us: are you the Messiah, the Son of God?"

Jesus replied, "The words are yours. But I tell you this: you will see the Son of Man seated at the right hand of God and coming on the clouds of heaven."

"Blasphemy!" said the High Priest. "Need we call any more witnesses. You have heard the blasphemy. What do you think of this?"

"Guilty. He should die," said the chief priests.

They took Jesus in chains to Pontius Pilate, the Governor. They said, "We found this man trying to cause trouble by telling people not to pay their taxes to Caesar, and claiming to be a Messiah, a king."

Pilate read out the charges, but Jesus did not say a word. He asked Jesus if he was King of the Jews. Jesus replied, "The words are yours."

Pilate could find nothing to prove the charges against Jesus.

It was the custom for the Governor to release a prisoner during the Passover. The Governor would ask the people whom he should release.

Pontius Pilate chose two prisoners, Jesus and Barabbas (who had led a rebellion and murdered someone). He turned to the crowd. Among them were people who, only a few days earlier, had thrown branches and cloaks on the ground before Jesus and hailed him as the Messiah. The chief priests were mingling with them, urging them to ask for Barabbas to be released.

"Which prisoner shall I release – Barabbas or Jesus the Messiah?"

"Barabbas!" shouted the crowd.

"Then what am I to do with Jesus the Messiah?" asked Pilate.

"Crucify him!" came the shout from the crowd.

"Why? What harm has he done?" asked Pilate.

"Crucify him!" shouted the crowd, over and over again. Pilate thought there was going be a riot. He took a jug of water and washed his hands in front of the people, saying, "My hands are clean of this man's blood; see to that yourselves."

Barabbas was freed and Jesus was nailed to a cross.

1 Why did the chief priests want to have Jesus killed?

Re-read page 24.

Think about the way in which the crowd had greeted Jesus when he came to Jerusalem.

> How did many people in Jerusalem think of Jesus?

> If Jesus became very popular with the people, what might happen to the chief priests?

2 What had happened to the people's feelings about Jesus by the time he was arrested?

Explain how this happened.

Discuss with a partner how a small group of people can influence a crowd. What kinds of things can happen because of this influence?

Write notes about some examples:

Event	Who influenced the people?	What happened?

3 In the Roman Empire, crucifixion was the way in which slaves and rebels were punished.

What happened when someone was crucified?

Why do you think this form of death was chosen for Jesus?

17 EASTER

The Resurrection

◀ This rock tomb, near a hill shaped like a skull, is said to be the one in which Joseph of Arimathea placed the body of Jesus.

The chief priests took Jesus to a hill called Golgotha ('the Place of the Skull'). They nailed him to a wooden cross. On it were written the words 'Jesus of Nazareth, King of the Jews'. Two criminals were crucified with him, one on each side. One of them made fun of him, but the other said, "Have you no fear of God? For us this is justice; we are paying the price for our crimes, but this man has done no wrong. Jesus, remember me when you come to your throne."

"I tell you this; today you shall be with me in Paradise," said Jesus.

At midday, darkness fell over the land; it lasted until three o'clock in the afternoon. The curtain in the temple ripped from top to bottom. Then Jesus gave a cry and said, "Father, into thy hands I commit my spirit." With those words he died.

A wealthy man named Joseph, from the town of Arimathea, believed that Jesus was innocent. He asked for his body, and it was given to him. Joseph wrapped the body of Jesus in a linen cloth and put it in the rock tomb he had prepared as his own. He rolled a great boulder in front of the entrance of the tomb.

Three women went to see the tomb; one of them was Mary, the mother of the disciple James. The next day they rested, because it was the Sabbath. On the Sunday they went to the tomb with oils and spices for anointing the body of Jesus.

The tomb was open. They went inside, but the body of Jesus had gone.

All of a sudden two men wearing dazzling white robes appeared. They said, "Why do you search among the dead for one who lives? Do you not remember what he said? He said that he must be given up to the power of sinful people and be crucified, but on the third day he would rise again."

The women went to find the disciples to tell them what they had seen and heard. The disciples would not believe them.

1 Describe the atmosphere among the women as they prepared the oils and set off to the tomb.

How did they feel when they found that the boulder had been moved, and then when they found the tomb empty?

How did they feel when the two men in dazzling white robes appeared?

2 What did Jesus mean when he answered the criminal who spoke to him?

3 The passage describes a mysterious event. What do you understand happened?

Support your answer with words from the text.

4 Christians believe in life after death.

Discuss this with your group.

Write down your ideas about what it might mean.

5 Find out more about the Resurrection from other sources.

Make notes about what you find out:

The Resurrection

Source	Facts	Christian beliefs

18 EASTER

Celebrating Easter

Easter can be thought of in sections:

Holy Week
(sometimes called Passiontide)
– the week leading up to the Crucifixion

Good Friday
– the day which commemorates the Crucifixion

Easter Sunday
– the day which commemorates the Resurrection (when the body of Jesus disappeared from his tomb and he reappeared as if alive).

This hymn is often sung in Christian churches at Easter.

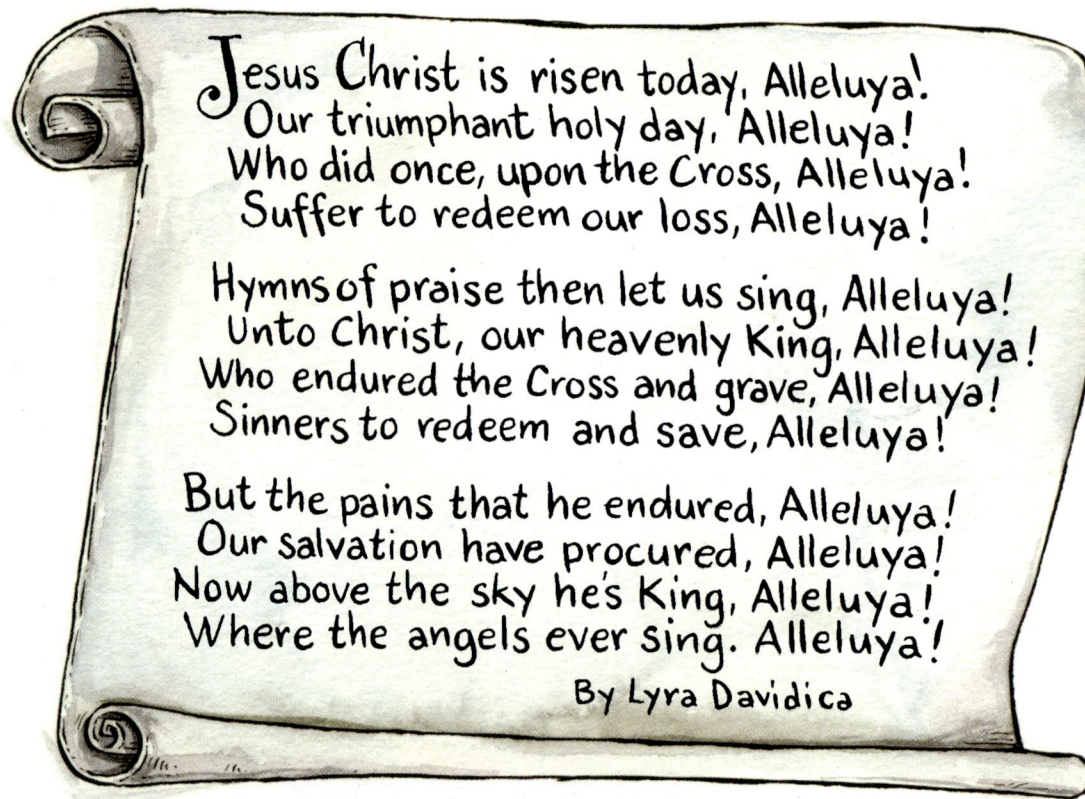

> Jesus Christ is risen today, Alleluya!
> Our triumphant holy day, Alleluya!
> Who did once, upon the Cross, Alleluya!
> Suffer to redeem our loss, Alleluya!
>
> Hymns of praise then let us sing, Alleluya!
> Unto Christ, our heavenly King, Alleluya!
> Who endured the Cross and grave, Alleluya!
> Sinners to redeem and save, Alleluya!
>
> But the pains that he endured, Alleluya!
> Our salvation have procured, Alleluya!
> Now above the sky he's King, Alleluya!
> Where the angels ever sing. Alleluya!
>
> By Lyra Davidica

1 Read the hymn and look up any words you do not understand.
With a partner, re-write the hymn in your own words (it need not rhyme or have the same rhythm).

2 What feelings does this hymn express?
Explain why Christians might want to show these feelings at Easter.

3 Think about the events leading up to the Crucifixion, and the Crucifixion itself. What feelings do these events create?

4 What kind of hymns do you think Christians might sing during Holy Week and on Good Friday?

How might the feelings of Christians change from Holy Week and Good Friday to Easter Sunday?

5 Crucifixes and plain crosses, like the ones in the pictures, can be seen in many Christian churches.

How might a crucifix or cross help Christians to worship?

6 Christians believe that Jesus died to save them from their sins, so that when they are forgiven for their sins they can have 'everlasting life'.

Write what you think these ideas might mean.

Discuss what happens to people when they die.

19 RELIGIONS IN YOUR NEIGHBOURHOOD

Looking for evidence

Evidence of religions in most areas can be found in maps, directories and on websites.

These sources show evidence of religions in Durham.

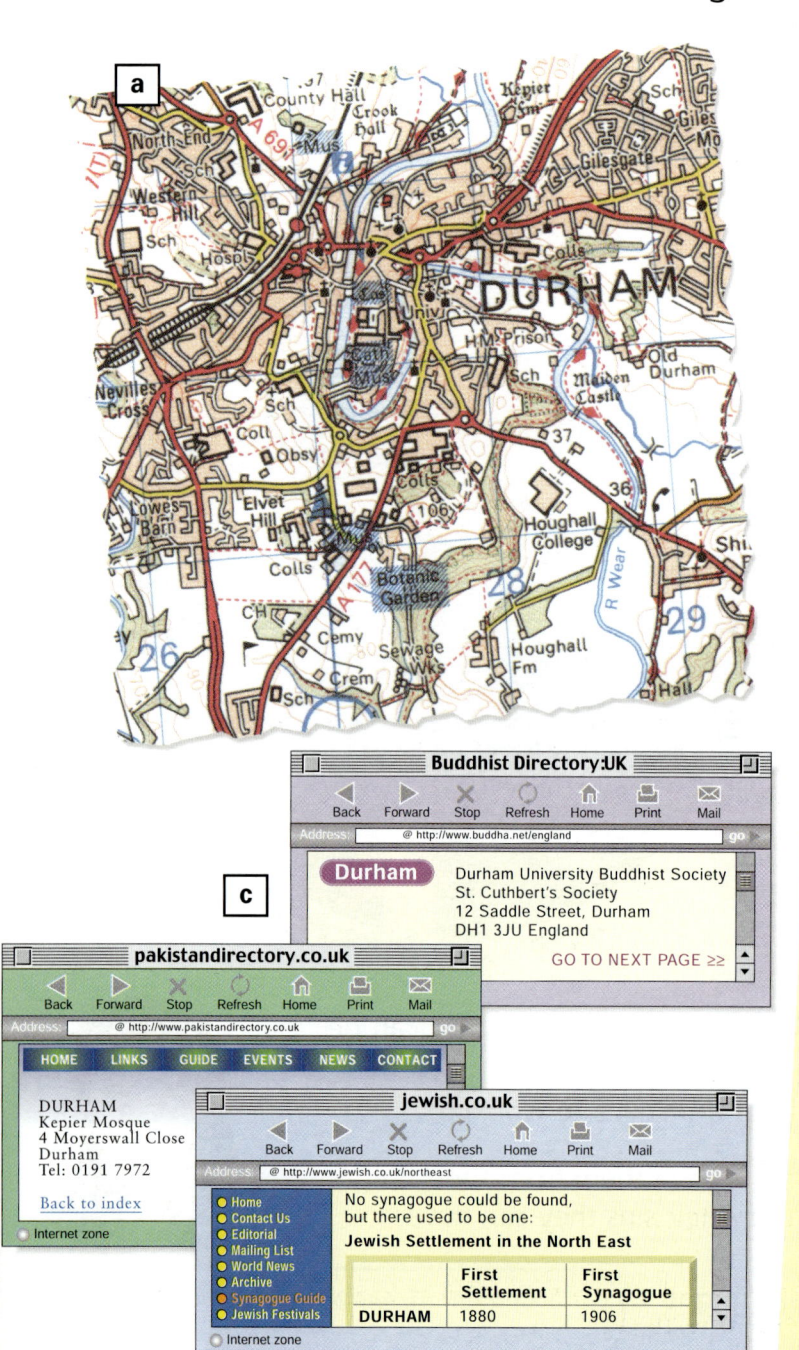

a [Map of Durham]

b THOMSON Directories™

PLACES OF WORSHIP

G	All Saints Church Carr House Dr Durham............0191-384 0143
	All Saints R C Church
	36 Kitswell Rd Lanchester Durham..............01207 520374
H	Carrville Methodist Church
	1 Grange Rd Durham..............................0191-386 8236
	Durham Cathedral The College Durham............0191-386 4266
I	Durham City Baptist Church Edge Ct Durham....0191-386 8476
	Elvet Methodist Church 8 Old Elvet Durham......0191-384 7599
	Emmanuel Church
J	96 Buckinghamshire Rd Durham..................0191-384 5624
	Methodist Chapel Cassop The Manse Linden Villa
	Coxhoe Durham......................................0191-377 0202
	Methodist Chapel Haswell
	The Manse Linden Villa Coxhoe Durham......0191-377 0202
	Nettlesworth Methodist Church
	Plawsworth Rd Sacriston Durham................0191-371 0337
K	Our Lady Of Mercy & St Godric R C Church
	Carr House Dr Durham..............................0191-384 3117
	Parkinson Memorial Methodist Church
	1 Grange Rd Durham..............................0191-386 8236
L	Phornoey Church
	The Manse Linden Villa Coxhoe Durham......0191-377 0202
	Pittington Methodist Church
	1 Grange Rd Durham..............................0191-386 8236
M	Queen Of Martyrs R C Church
	Newhouse Rd Esh Winning Durham............0191-373 4340
	Sacriston Methodist Church
	Front St Sacriston Durham........................0191-371 0337
N	Salvation Army The
	Lansbury Dr Birtley Chester Le Street............0191-410 2807
	Plawsworth Rd Sacriston Durham..............0191-371 0001
	49 Saddler St Durham............................0191-384 6901
O	Sherburn Methodist Church
	1 Grange Rd Durham..............................0191-386 8236
	St Andrews C Of E Church Church Bank Stanley..01207 233936
	St Andrews Methodist
	The Manse Linden Villa Coxhoe Durham......0191-377 0202
P	St Andrews Methodist Park Church
	Front St Langley Park Durham
	Carr Av Brandon Durham..........................0191-371 0337
	The Manse 25 Cavendish Ct Brandon Durham..0191-378 2294
	Stanley Methodist Church Circuit
	33 Ford Rd Lanchester Durham..................0191-378 9555
Q	St Bedes Front St Sacriston Durham..............01207 520604
	St Bede's R C Church Sacriston Durham..........0191-371 0257
	St Benet R C Church Tenter Terr Durham........0191-384 3117
	St Brandons Parochial Church Brancepeth
R	Durham..0191-410 2923
	St Cuthbert R C Church
	Ropery La Chester Le Street......................0191-378 3596
	Old Elvet Durham..................................0191-388 2302
S	St Johns Church Nevilles Cross Durham..........0191-384 3442
	St Joseph R C Church
	Birtley La Birtley Chester Le Street..............0191-383 9181
	St Josephs Church
T	Durham Rd Ushaw Moor Durham................0191-410 2923
	St Joseph's Presbytery Mill La Durham............0191-373 0219
	St Margarets C Of E Church
	Crossgate Durham..................................0191-384 3810
U	St Mary Magdalene C Of E Church
	Belmont Vicarage Broomside La
	Durham..0191-384 3623
	St Mary's Catholic Church South Moor Stanley..01207 232798
	St Mary & St Cuthbert C Of E Church
V	Parish Centre Church Chare Chester Le Street..0191-388 3295
	St Mary The Virgin C Of E Church
	89 Front St Sherburn Durham....................0191-372 2797
	St Michael & All Angels C Of E Church
W	Dene Bank Witton Gilbert Durham..............0191-371 0376
	St Michaels R C Church Esh Durham............0191-373 4349
	St Nicholas C Of E Church
	Kepier Villas Durham
	St Patricks Church North Rd Dipton Stanley......0191-384 1180
X	St Patrick's R C Church
	High Street South Langley Moor Durham......01207 570209
	St Paul's C Of E Church
	Russell St Waterhouses Durham..................0191-378 0057
	West Pelton Stanley..............................0191-373 4273
Y	St Paul's Methodist Church..........................0191-370 2146
	St Teresa's Church
	Ceiloe The Manse Linden Villa Coxhoe Durham..0191-377 0202
	James St Annfield Plain Stanley..................01207 234388
Z	Waddington Street United Reformed Church
	3 Waddington St Durham..........................0191-386 0604
	Witton Gilbert Methodist Church
	Sacriston La Witton Gilbert Durham............0191-371 0337

c Buddhist Directory:UK
http://www.buddha.net/england
Durham — Durham University Buddhist Society
St. Cuthbert's Society
12 Saddle Street, Durham
DH1 3JU England
GO TO NEXT PAGE ≫

pakistandirectory.co.uk
http://www.pakistandirectory.co.uk
HOME | LINKS | GUIDE | EVENTS | NEWS | CONTACT
DURHAM
Kepier Mosque
4 Moyerswall Close
Durham
Tel: 0191 7972
Back to index

jewish.co.uk
http://www.jewish.co.uk/northeast
- Home
- Contact Us
- Editorial
- Mailing List
- World News
- Archive
- Synagogue Guide
- Jewish Festivals

No synagogue could be found, but there used to be one:

Jewish Settlement in the North East

	First Settlement	First Synagogue
DURHAM	1880	1906

40

1 What do sources a and b tell you about the religions in Durham?
You could write on a chart:

Religions in Durham			
Source a		Source b	
Religion	Evidence	Religion	Evidence

Write a summary of religions in Durham, based on these two sources.

2 Look at source c. What can you find out from it about religions in Durham?
From sources a, b and c, what would you expect to see during a walk around the area?

3 Which religion seems to be the most common among people of this city?
How can you tell?

4 List any religions which cannot be found in the evidence.
Does this mean that there are no people from those religions there?
What other evidence could you use to find out?

5 The religions in a neighbourhood sometimes change.
How can you find out if this has happened?
What might cause these changes?
How can you find out if your explanations are right?

What kinds of evidence would help you?

6 Use directories, maps, websites and other texts, and people you know, to find evidence for religions in your neighbourhood.

20 RELIGIONS IN YOUR NEIGHBOURHOOD

Buildings

These photographs were taken in Durham.

a

b **ELVET METHODIST CHURCH**

Minister		Church Services
Rev. J.L.H. Allison B.Sc.	8.30 a.m.	Holy Communion – Second Sundays
Tel. No. 384 8755	10.40 a.m.	Creche and Junior Church
	10.45 a.m.	Morning Worship
Deacon. E. Timmins	6.00 p.m.	Evening Worship
Tel. No. 377 8089		Methsoc
	7.30 p.m.	In University Terms

c

e ← St Cuthbert's RC Church

d **dhoon dhamaka** – an explosion of music and dance
Friday 1 March 2002 • 7pm for 7:30pm
National Hindu Students Forum North Zone proudly presents
£24 members
£27 non members

f

▲ **Kepier Mosque**

42

1. What do photographs a, b, c, d, e and f tell you about religions in Durham? Explain your answers.

   Describe what you can see in the photographs.

2. Re-read the evidence from pages 40 and 41 about religions in Durham. How did a walk around the city help to find evidence of religions there?

3. Make a chart on which to record the evidence of all the religions in Durham:

Religion	Any evidence? ✔ or ✘	Type of evidence
Buddhism		
Christianity		

   What other sources of evidence could have been used?

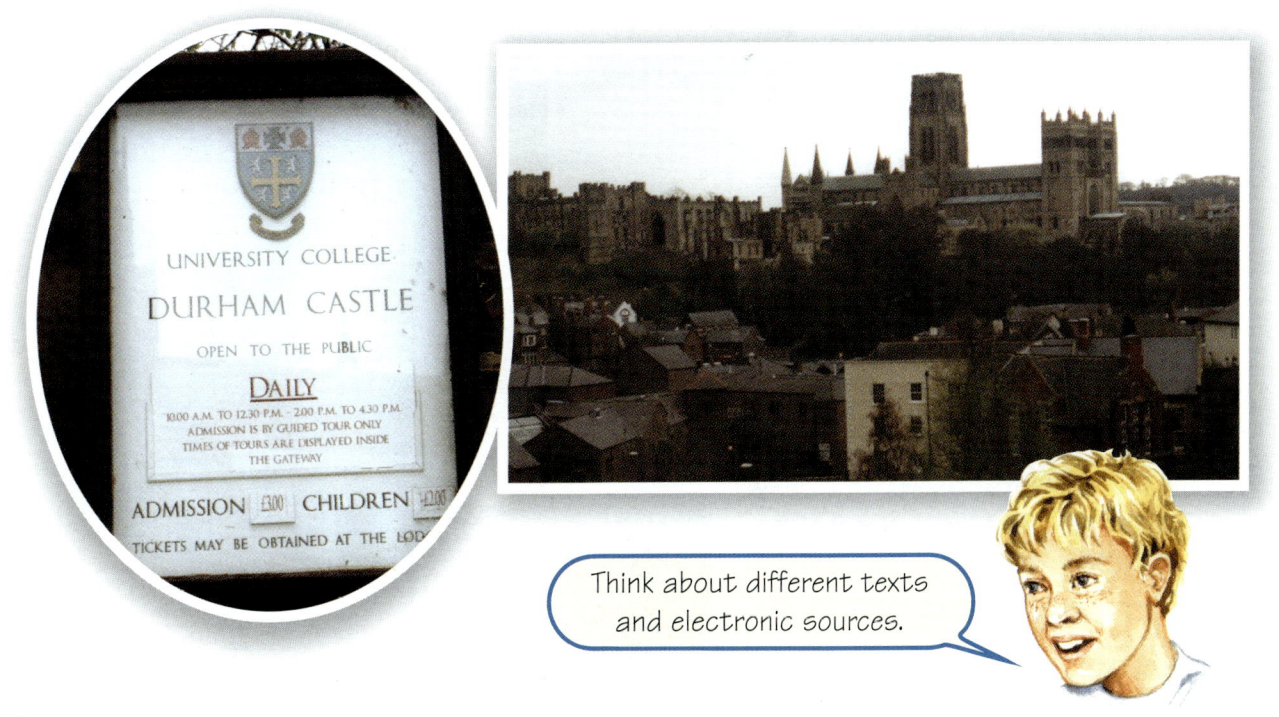

   Think about different texts and electronic sources.

4. Which religions do not appear to have a place of worship in Durham? For which of these religions is there some evidence? Explain why they might have no place of worship.

5. Look around your neighbourhood for evidence of religions.

21 RELIGIONS IN YOUR NEIGHBOURHOOD

Caring and sharing

Religious groups have different ways of helping people in need and of sharing with others.

a ▼ Christianity

b ▲ Sikhism

c ▲ Judaism

THEY'RE NOT ASKING FOR A TON OF MONEY TO SURVIVE THE WINTER. JUST A TON OF COAL.

d ▲ Buddhism

e ◀ Islam

44

1 What evidence can you find in the pictures of religious groups helping people or sharing? You could write on a chart:

Source	Religion	People giving help	People receiving help
a			
b			

Use information texts.

From Sources a to f, describe the ways in which the different religious groups help people.

2 Some religions have a special word for giving or sharing.
Find out about zakah in Islam and tzedakah in Judaism.

3 List other ways in which anyone can give or share.

- What can be given or shared?
- To whom can it be given?
- What difference will it make?

4 Collect information about the ways in which religious groups care for and share with others in your neighbourhood.
Find evidence from as many sources as you can:

Leaflets **Posters** **Local radio** **Websites** **Newspapers** **Magazines**

Record your findings on a table:

Event or action	Religious group	What is given	To whom it is given

45

22 RELIGIONS IN YOUR NEIGHBOURHOOD

Similarities and differences

This 'religious trail', based on the neighbourhood of one school, helps visitors and other pupils to find out about the religious groups in the area. For each label on the map there is an information file. The reader can go to the information file to find out more about each place which is labelled.

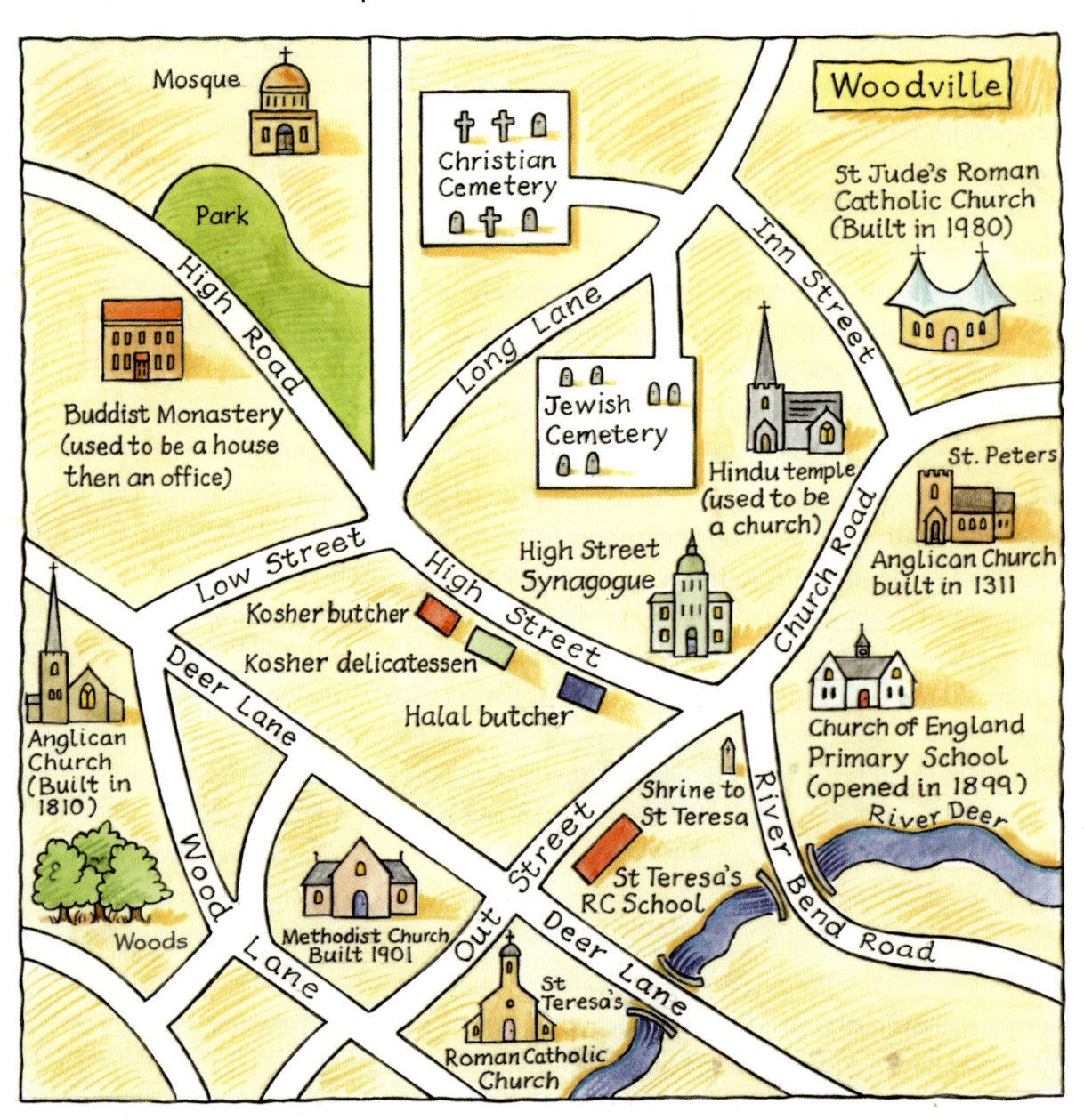

Census data: numbers of people

Religion	1801 (Total population 1706)	1901 (Total population 2999)	2001 (Total population 4105)
Buddhist	0	0	201
Christian	1631	2450	1801
Hindu	0	0	306
Jewish	75	460	954
Muslim	0	65	206
Sikh	0	0	106
None	0	24	531

1 Which religions are present in the area now? How can you tell?

Religion	Evidence

2 Which is the oldest religion in the area?

What is the evidence for this?

3 Make notes about the changes in religion between 1801 and 2001. Use evidence from the religious trail.

Write a short report about these changes.

4 Write directions to tell visitors to the area about what they will see of different religions there.

Welcome to Woodville

Many different religions can be found in Woodville. Some have special places of worship. Others meet in people's homes.

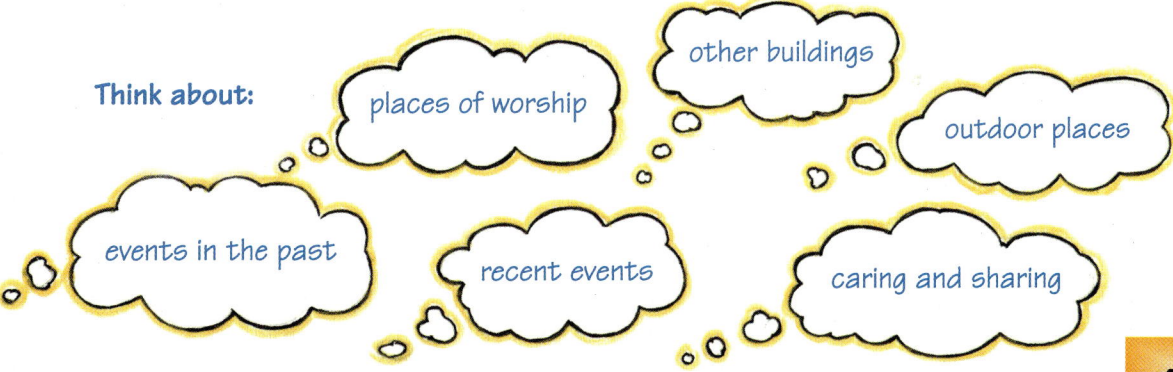

5 Make a religious trail for your neighbourhood.

6 Compare your neighbourhood with Woodville (page 46). What similarities can you see?

Think about:
- places of worship
- other buildings
- outdoor places
- events in the past
- recent events
- caring and sharing

Glossary

alleluya	A word used in hymns meaning 'praise the Lord'.	**mandir**	A Hindu temple.
anoint	Pour or rub on holy oil.	**manger**	A trough for animals' food.
arti	A Hindu **ceremony** in which lamps, bells and incense are used to welcome a god or goddess.	**Messiah**	The one the prophets said would save people from their **sins**. It means 'the **anointed** one'.
betel	A climbing evergreen shrub.	**minister**	A Christian priest or vicar.
betray	To give someone up to an enemy.	**murti**	A statue or picture of a Hindu god or goddess.
blasphemy	Talking about something sacred in a bad way.	**myrrh**	A perfume made from a gum from trees.
census	A count of the population.	**Nativity**	The birth of Jesus.
ceremony	A formal act of worship.	**Palm Sunday**	The day which **commemorates** the time when Jesus went to Jerusalem and people threw palm leaves onto the ground in front of him.
commemorate	To keep in memory.		
Communion	The Christian service in which bread and wine represent (or become) the body and blood of Christ. Also **Eucharist** and **Lord's Supper**.		
		Paradise	Heaven.
		Passover	A Jewish festival which commemorates an event told in the Old Testament.
covenant	A promise or pact.		
crucifix	A cross on which there is an image of Jesus.	**pilgrim**	Someone who goes on a religious journey.
Crucifixion	When Jesus was nailed to the cross.	**prophet**	Someone to whom God speaks and who tells others the word of God.
crucify	To nail someone onto a cross.	**puja**	Hindu worship.
Easter	The Christian festival which celebrates the **Resurrection** of Christ.	**redeem**	To save or rescue.
		Resurrection	When Jesus returned to life after he died.
endure	To suffer.	**Sabbath**	For Christians and Jews a holy day of rest.
Eucharist	See **Communion** and **Lord's Supper**; the elements of bread and wine used within the communion service.		
		salvation	Saving.
		shrine	A holy place in which people worship. A shrine is usually dedicated to a person or being, such as a Christian saint or a Hindu deity.
frankincense	A sweet smelling incense.		
Ganges	A river in India which is sacred to Hindus.		
Good Friday	The day which **commemorates** the **Crucifixion** of Christ.	**sin**	A wrong or bad action, or to do something wrong or bad.
grotto	A cave.	**thy**	An old word meaning 'your'.
Holy Week	The week leading up to **Easter**.	**tzedakah**	Giving to charity in Judaism.
incense	Solid perfume which is burned.	**Upanishads**	Hindu scriptures.
kum-kum	A red powder used by Hindus to put a mark on the forehead to symbolise good health and to show that a person is ready to take part in worship.	**veena**	A stringed musical instrument.
		vermilion	Deep red.
		zakah	A payment by Muslims to help others. It is seen as a way of purifying any wealth they have.
langar	The kitchen and eating area of a gurdwara (a Sikh temple).		
Lord's Supper	See **Communion**.		
lotus flower	A pink and white flower; a symbol of purity to Hindus.		